E; 9?
LAZ

90124
A

CHARLES P. LAZARUS

The Titan
of
Toys "R" Us

CHARLES P. LAZARUS

The Titan

of

Toys "R" Us

Anne Koopman

GEC GARRETT EDUCATIONAL CORPORATION

Cover: *Charles P. Lazarus.* (Toys "R" Us.)

Manufactured in the United States of America

Edited and produced by Synthegraphics Corporation

Library of Congress Cataloging-in-Publication Data

Koopman, Anne.
    Charles P. Lazarus : the titan of Toys "R" Us / Anne Koopman.
        p. cm. — (Wizards of business)
    Includes index.
    Summary: A biography of the World War II veteran who began a baby furniture business which blossomed into a worldwide concern.
    ISBN 1-56074-022-1
    1. Lazarus, Charles P., 1926-   —Juvenile literature.
2. Businessmen—United States—Biography—Juvenile literature.
3. Toy industry—United States—Juvenile literature.   [1. Lazarus, Charles P., 1926-   .   2. Businessmen.]   I. Title.   II. Series.
HD9993.T962L395   1991
381'.4568872'092—dc20   91-32054
[B]   CIP
                                                                 AC

Contents

Chronology for *Charles P. Lazarus*

1923	Born on October 4 in Washington, D.C.
1948	Opened baby furniture store
1950	Began to stock baby toys
1957	Opened first store called Toys "R" Us
1966	Four stores in Washington, D.C., area had total sales of 12 million dollars a year; sold chain to Interstate Stores but continued to run Toys "R" Us
1974	Interstate filed for bankruptcy; Lazarus appointed by court to run Interstate
1978	Led Interstate out of bankruptcy; reorganized company and renamed it Toys "R" Us
1983	Kids "R" Us clothing stores opened
1984	Toys "R" Us opened in Canada, England, and Singapore
1989	Toys "R" Us had 404 stores in the United States, 74 abroad, and 137 Kids "R" Us stores in the United States
1991	Toys "R" Us joined with McDonald's to open a combined store in Japan

Chapter 1

"Give the Customers What They Want"

There were many important moments and decisions in his early business years that put Charles Lazarus onto the road to success. He quickly learned to give his customers what they wanted, and to sell items for a lower price than the competition as well as in a more convenient way.

But there is one decision that Lazarus thinks contributed the most to his success. After he had opened two stores that sold baby furniture and toys, he noticed that those customers who came in to buy toys always returned to buy more toys. Those customers who had bought baby furniture, however, rarely came back to buy more furniture. Customers who came back again and again, or "repeat customers," are the basis of most successful businesses.

TOYS BREAK!

Lazarus wondered why only the toy customers kept coming back. Then the answer came to him. It was simple: toys break! Moreover, children always need new toys to replace those that wear out or go out of fashion, or they have outgrown their old toys and want new ones.

Baby furniture, on the other hand, rarely breaks or wears out. Most families use the same crib or high chair over again for each new baby. "Furniture lasts forever," Charles has pointed out, "but toys . . . are great to sell because they have built-in **obsolescence.** Kids break them." (Terms in **boldface type** are defined in the Glossary at the back of this book.)

Based on this observation. Lazarus decided that his stores would primarily sell toys. The stores would offer a wide variety of items in a **self-service,** supermarket style and at a **discount.** He would still sell baby furniture and other related items, but this **merchandise** would no longer be the main attraction in any of his stores.

With this decision, a whole new way of selling toys was born, and Charles Philip Lazarus was on his way to fame and fortune.

GETTING STARTED

Like so many other young men, Charles Lazarus served in the armed forces during World War II. After he was discharged from the Army, he returned to his family's home in Washington, D.C., where his father owned a small shop, dusty and crowded with used bicycles.

For as long as Lazarus could remember, his father bought old, broken bicycles. He repaired and painted them, then sold them for a **profit.** The Lazarus family lived in an apartment above the shop, where Charles, one of several children, had been born on October 4 in 1923.

The Bike Shop's "Business Education"

From the time he was a baby, Charles Lazarus spent a great deal of time in his father's bicycle shop. He even claims he learned to walk and ride a tricycle on about the same day he was born. When he was older, Charles helped his father fix the bikes and serve customers. He also had ideas to improve the business.

For example, Charles often wondered why his father didn't sell new bikes. "Wouldn't that bring in more customers and make more profit?" he asked. His father said it was better for a small shop to stick to used bikes because bigger stores could sell new bikes so much cheaper.

Charles didn't quite understand why this should be. His father explained that a larger store could buy more bikes at one time. Therefore, a bike **manufacturer** would lower the price for a large order, or sell at a discount for quantity.

While Charles and his father continued to repair and sell used bikes, Charles would often daydream about growing up and having a store of his own.

TWO GOALS

Charles Lazarus was in his early twenties when he left the Army. He wasn't sure exactly what he wanted to do with his life. Although the government offered financial aid for college to former servicemen, Lazarus wasn't interested in spending the next four years studying for a college diploma. Ambitious and hardworking, he knew one thing: "I wanted to work and I wanted to make money."

Lazarus knew from the start that he wanted to work for himself, probably in **retailing.** "The Army . . . was my one experience with being part of an organization, and after that I decided that I wanted to work for myself." His father had been an important example for him, and Lazarus had gained a lot of business training from his years around the bicycle shop.

Lazarus thought that he could sell some product out of his father's shop. If he was successful enough, he would then open his own store. But what should that product be? He thought a lot about it, looking around and listening to the conversations of his father's customers and people he knew.

"What do people want?" Charles asked himself. "What do people need?" He tried looking into the future to figure out what products the public would need more and more. He wanted to find a **market** that had growth possibilities.

A Smart Guess

As he looked around for ideas, Charles saw young men, much like himself, who had recently been discharged from the Army. Many of these men were newly married and starting to raise families. Charles guessed that there would soon be a big demand for baby furniture.

As Charles once said, "I chose baby furniture because after the war I could see that a lot of people were getting married, and so I thought there would be a lot of babies. I suppose I anticipated the baby boom."

Charles' guess was right. During the postwar years of the late forties and early fifties, more babies were born than ever before in the country's history. In 1948, when he was twenty-two years old, Charles borrowed $2,000 and started his first business, selling baby furniture.

"My first shop was 40 feet by 60 feet," Charles recalls, "and it was filled with cribs and baby furniture. I was there from 8:00 A.M. until 9:00 P.M., six and seven days a week. I did everything myself, even delivering the furniture to customers."

When Charles wasn't delivering furniture, he was busy helping customers, taking orders, ordering merchandise from manufacturers, keeping track of **inventory,** and doing **billing.**

GIVING CUSTOMERS WHAT THEY WANT

Lazarus recalls that he had been selling furniture for about two years when one day a woman asked him, "Don't you have any toys for my baby?" He had to reply that he was sorry, he didn't stock toys, only furniture.

When the customer left, Lazarus realized that she hadn't been the first person to ask for toys. Many other customers had asked the same question, and Charles always had to give the same answer. But on that day in 1950, for some reason, Charles finally got the message: *The customers want toys.*

Realizing that simple fact, Charles claims, was a very important business lesson for him. "If you want to succeed, you have to give the customers what they want."

Aiming to do just that, Lazarus ordered a few toys for his shop and began to sell them along with the baby furniture. The first toys he stocked were for infants and toddlers. One was a cradle gym that ran across the baby's crib; another hooked onto the playpen.

As his customers' children grew and their needs became more varied, the merchandise in Charles' shop became more varied, too. After a few years, he began to sell tricycles, books, and a much wider range of toys. His business was growing, and so were the number and kinds of toys he carried.

Chapter 2

A Toy Supermarket

While on a trip to New York City a couple of years later, Lazarus happened to visit a store that also sold baby furniture. But this store sold the furniture in a different way and for lower prices.

The store in New York was set up like a supermarket, where customers had a wide selection of items and basically served themselves, a style of retail **merchandising** known as self-service. The store made a big impression on Charles. He went back to Washington with ideas about a whole new direction for his business.

A FASCINATION WITH SELF-SERVICE

Charles was fascinated by the success of the self-service grocery supermarkets of the early 1950s. He observed the operations of these stores and considered the advantages that this method of retailing offered to both the customer and the store owner. He decided to apply the same basic principles of the supermarket to his own baby furniture and toy shop.

Charles reorganized his store, modeling it after a supermarket. One way he did this was by stocking more items and a wider variety of each item. For example, in his old store, he may have had in stock only one or two styles of baby cribs. If a customer wanted one of the cribs, Charles would order it from the manufacturer and then deliver the crib to the customer when it came in. The crib might take as long as six weeks to reach the customer.

In his new store, Charles had many different styles of cribs and a number of each in stock. When a customer chose a particular crib, Charles could deliver it immediately. And by ordering in larger quantities from the manufacturer, he was able to get each item at a reduced price. He could then sell the items at a lower price to his customers and still make a profit.

A New Name

Customers now served themselves in the new store. Since the store was self-service, Charles did not have to pay a large staff of salespeople. That savings in **overhead** costs also helped make it possible to sell the items at a discount.

The store was now much different in the merchandise it offered customers, and in the way it offered that merchandise. Charles thought he needed a new name to communicate these changes to the public. He had always believed that a store name should be simple and should tell the customer exactly what the store had to offer. He decided to change the name of his store to Baby Furniture and Toy Supermarket.

A Second Store and Another Important Lesson

Soon after reorganizing his first store, Lazarus opened another one. An empty supermarket proved to be a perfect site because it had all the space he needed for a large selection of merchandise. Customers could even use carts to serve themselves. The opening of his second store was a very happy day for Charles. His hard work and ambition were now paying off.

With the opening of his second store, Charles quickly became aware that it was impossible for him to be in both stores at the same time. He now had to learn how to direct other people to run the stores while he was not there. He had to train them and rely on them.

When he had first started out, Charles did everything himself. But now he realized that if he wanted his business to keep on growing, he had to build upon solid business **systems** and **management.** This phase of his business education provided another important lesson for him.

A NEW FOCUS, ANOTHER NEW NAME

The name of his two stores, Baby Furniture and Toy Supermarket, was no longer an accurate description of the merchandise Charles had to offer. He decided on a shorter name, something catchy that would say it all. In 1957 he opened the first store that featured mainly toys and called it Toys "R" Us, spelling the name with the "R" reversed.

Geoffrey the Giraffe (left), the Toys "R" Us mascot, and some of the other animal characters used by the company to entertain customers. (Toys "R" Us.)

Charles had always reversed the R's in the spelling of Baby Furniture and Toy Supermarket, trying to give the impression that a young child might have written it that way. Now he did the same in his new name, creating a distinctive **logo** for his company. Throughout the years, Lazarus has received many complaints from school teachers and well-intentioned customers about the spelling "mistake". But Charles knew that the clever "twist" made shoppers notice and remember the name of his stores. What more could a merchant ask for?

Years later, Geoffrey the Giraffe would become the company's "mascot." The friendly looking Geoffrey would also create a memorable, positive impression with shoppers.

Chapter 3

A Formula for Success

When Charles Lazarus opened his first Toys "R" Us store in 1957, the entire toy industry was much different from the way it is now. There were far fewer companies making toys in the United States, and toys were sold in a much different way. In part, the tremendous success of Toys "R" Us was due to Lazarus' pioneering of a new way to sell toys and foreseeing that the toy market would grow beyond anyone's wildest dreams.

A SEASONAL BUSINESS

When Charles Lazarus first started selling toys in 1950, they were sold either in small shops or in the toy departments of large department stores. In order to compete with the department stores, the small shops tended to specialize in the kinds of toys they sold. Some, for example, would sell only toys for toddlers, while others sold only toys for children of grade-school age.

Toys were a seasonal business. Both the small shops and department stores sold the vast amount of their toys around the Christmas holidays. The department stores would expand their toy sections, fill them with holiday stock, and most would even hire a Santa Claus to draw customer traffic in the right direction.

Toy prices were marked up for maximum profit during the Christmas holidays. But right after Christmas, the prices on any leftover items were reduced and sold off at big discounts in order to clear out the stock. After Christmas, department stores carried a sparse selection of toys, which seemed to suit the limited demand for toy items during the rest of the year.

A BOOM IN BABIES AND TOYS

In the 1950s, there were also far fewer types of toys available. There was nowhere near the thousands of toy items now manufactured in the United States and abroad.

Before World War II, most lower priced toys were made in Japan. Many of these Japanese products were poorly constructed, made of inferior materials with sharp edges and pieces that broke off. Finely crafted toys were manufactured in Germany and other European countries. However, these toys were usually too expensive for the average person to afford.

With the postwar baby boom, more American manufacturers jumped into the business of making toys. It made good business sense. Because of the large increase in the number of American children, there was a greater need for toys.

Parents were also spending much more money on toys for their children than did parents of previous generations. Lazarus observed that parents of the postwar era seemed to be saying, "Hey, I didn't have those things when I was a kid, but I want my kid to have them."

Toys also became less and less of a seasonal item. Parents were more likely to buy toys all year 'round, instead of only at holidays or for birthdays.

All of these factors combined to create a demand for more toys and a greater variety of toys.

Toys at a Reasonable Price

Charles Lazarus has said that he has always tried to "serve the customer's needs." It has always been clear to Lazarus that "the first thing the customer wanted was price."

Even as a boy, working in his father's shop, Charles noticed that the most important question customers asked was, "What's the price on this bike?" They wanted to find the best buy for their money, whether it was a bike, baby furniture, or a teddy bear.

This may seem like a very obvious observation. It only makes sense that customers want a bargain. However, the merchant must then figure out how to sell an item at the lowest possible price and still make an adequate profit.

Charles figured out several ways to sell toys at a discount. One way was to buy large quantities of an item from the manufacturer, another was to keep the cost of running the business, or overhead, as low as possible.

SQUEEZING OUT A PROFIT IN LEMON TOWN

In order to understand how Lazarus did this, imagine that you live in Lemon Town and decide to open a lemonade stand. You call it "Super Lemonade" and you guess that each week you can sell at least 200 cups of lemonade. But how much should you charge for each cup in order to make the most profit? You're not sure.

Calculating Costs

First, you must figure out how much it costs to make the lemonade (adding in the cost of lemons, sugar, jars, etc.). Then you must add the cost of paper cups to serve it and the salary of three people you want to hire to wait on customers. There is also the cost of advertising in the local newspaper.

Then there is the cost of building your stand. Maybe you can find an old table for free to use as the stand. But you want to decorate it with brightly colored helium balloons that you need to buy each week. This cost must also be added to your list of expenses.

You finally figure out that your lemonade stand will cost twenty dollars a week in overhead to run. Therefore, if you sell 200 cups of lemonade at ten cents a cup (200 X .10 = $20), you will just break even, or only cover the overhead costs. In order to make a profit, you must charge more than ten cents a cup. Every penny over that amount will be your profit.

You now decide to charge twenty cents a cup, which is the usual price of lemonade at all the other stands in Lemon Town. The first week, business is booming. You sell 200 cups of lemonade and make ten cents a cup in profit. That's twenty dollars in your pocket.

But the next week, business is terrible! You find out that all your customers are going around the corner to a new stand that sells lemonade for only ten cents a cup! Ten cents a cup? You can't believe it, so you go around the corner to investigate the competition.

It's true. There's a lemonade stand with a line of customers. A big sign above it says, "Lemonade-For-Less."

The Secret of Success at Lemonade-For-Less

How do they do it? You can't understand how Lemonade-For-Less can make any profit selling their product at only ten cents a cup. Why, is costs you (and all the other lemonade stands in town) that much just to break even.

Then you find out how the other vendor figured out how to reduce his overhead and sell his lemonade at a discount. First, he doesn't have a lot of salespeople at his stand to wait on customers like you do. He keeps the lemonade in a big jug and the customers serve themselves. He only needs one salesperson to collect the money and fill the jug when it becomes empty. Therefore, his overhead does not include the cost of these extra salaries.

Your competitor serves his lemonade in paper cups, just like you do. But he buys plain white cups, which are much cheaper than the fancy, colored cups that you use. His overhead doesn't include the higher cost for fancy cups.

He also got a table for free to use as his stand, just like you did. But he doesn't decorate it. His stand is certainly not as attractive as yours, but his overhead doesn't include the cost of such frills as helium balloons.

Most importantly, it costs your competitor less to make his lemonade, even though he buys his lemons and sugar at the same supermarket you do. How does he do it? The reason is that he buys the ingredients in much larger quantities than you and has negotiated a discount price with the supermarket for his large-volume orders.

When your competitor adds up the cost of doing business for one week, his overhead is much lower than yours. It costs him only ten dollars a week to run his stand, which is half the cost of your overhead. Therefore, if he sells 200 cups of lemonade per week, he can charge much less per cup and still make a good profit.

Lemonade-For-Less Takes Over

The first week that Lemonade-For-Less opened, it charged ten cents per cup and sold 200 cups. The **gross revenue** from these sales was twenty dollars. After the owner subtracted his overhead, his **net revenue,** or profit, was ten dollars.

The second week, the news of your competitor's low-priced lemonade spread through Lemon Town. He sold 400 cups at ten cents a cup and did forty dollars worth of business. Subtracting ten dollars for his overhead, he made a profit of thirty dollars that week.

Unfortunately, because he attracted so many customers in the neighborhood with his low prices, your competitor put you out of business. The next week, Lemonade-For-Less did so well that the owner used his successful formula and his profits to open a second stand—right on the same corner where your stand used to be!

At Lemonade-For-Less, the owner decided that the customers he wanted to attract didn't care about special service, or buying lemonade from a nicely decorated stand. His customers only wanted a low price. He figured out a way to keep his overhead down so he could sell his lemonade at a low price and still make a good profit.

BUYING IN QUANTITY, SELLING AT A DISCOUNT

Lazarus was also able to sell items for less than his competitors because he bought larger quantities from the manufacturer and could negotiate a lower price. He was able to buy in large quantities because each of his stores was designed to hold more stock than most other toy stores. Also, unlike department stores, Lazarus sold toys year 'round instead of just at Christmas. He kept his inventory in a large warehouse and restocked his shelves with items as necessary.

Consider, for example, a small toy shop that might order ten dollhouses from the Doll World Company. The shop might be charged the **wholesale** price of ten dollars per house, or $100 for the ten houses. In order to make any profit, the shop must price the dollhouses above ten dollars. The shop cannot order any more than ten houses because there is not enough storage space for stock. Also, there are not that many customers for dollhouses passing through the small store.

However, right after Christmas the Doll World Company needs to sell out the current model of its dollhouse to make way for next year's model. They are willing to give a discount on the wholesale price for any large-volume orders. If a store orders 100 dollhouses, Doll World will charge eight dollars for each house. But if the store orders 200 houses, the company will reduce the cost of each house to six dollars. For an order of 300 houses, Doll World will charge only four dollars per house.

Therefore, if Toys "R" Us bought 300 dollhouses, they could sell them for slightly more than four dollars each and still make a good profit.

THE BIGGEST SELECTION

What else does the customer want besides a low price? Charles Lazarus thought that the second most important attraction for customers was a large selection of merchandise. That is another reason he found the supermarket-style stores ideal for the way he wanted to sell toys.

When a customer came in to buy a baby stroller, Lazarus noticed that the person wanted to see as many baby strollers made as possible. The customer would compare the price, construction, and style, then finally choose one. Of course, the customer might shop around in different stores, comparing strollers, and end up finding a stroller at some other store.

Lazarus decided that if people knew he had *every* different style of stroller available, they would come to his store. They would see the biggest selection of strollers all in one place and save time. As Lazarus has noted, "We don't just buy one line; we buy everything. So if you want to buy a stroller, we have a hundred strollers. Now, you want to buy only one, but want to see it all. That's how people are."

As the toy industry grew, manufacturing more toys each

One of the keys to the success of Toys "R" Us is always having available a large supply of all the items that the company sells. (NYT Pictures.)

year, the aisles at Toys "R" Us were stocked with an ever-widening selection. Striving to provide customers with the biggest selection of toys proved to be an important part of the company's successful formula. At the present time, the Toys "R" Us chain offers customers almost 20,000 items in each store.

Attracting "Traffic"

Another way that Lazarus figured out how to attract customers— especially in the non-holiday season—was to sell some standard, essential item at an outrageous discount. The item he chose was disposable diapers, and his stores are known for selling Pampers at rock-bottom prices.

In every Toys "R" Us store, the Pampers are stocked far away from the cash registers. Therefore, shoppers have to walk through the entire store before they can get to the diapers. When shoppers—and any children with them—pass all that merchandise, they are bound to come out of the stores with more than a package of diapers.

HAVING IT ON HAND

Lazarus found that another important attraction for customers was simply having an adequate supply of an item the customer wanted. He imagined a shopper with a list of ten items. In many stores, the shopper would only find five of the items on his list. He would have to go to other stores to find the other items, a task that would take him much more time.

Lazarus believes it is crucial for his stores to have a large supply of all the items they sell. By using a very complex computerized system, the inventory stays on pace with sales. This greatly reduces the chances of a customer not finding the item he wants on the shelves.

"When a customer walks into our store with a list of ten items, we hope to have all ten," says Lazarus. "If we have nine, I guess we are satisfied. If we have eight, I'm very unhappy. That means the customer has to go somewhere else and find the other two."

BEATING OUT THE GIANTS

Lazarus has strived to develop business methods that offer his customers the best price, selection, and inventory of any retail toy merchant. In doing so, he has clearly beat out all competition, including the department store giants.

Lazarus has described his competition with department stores in this way: "Department stores have such overhead that they simply cannot compete with what we are able to do. We can sell [an item] at a much lower price. What we have is more of a distribution system. What we've done more than anything else is to get the merchandise from the manufacturer to our register at the least possible cost."

Chapter 4

Some Ups and Downs

Soon after the first Toys "R" Us store opened in 1957, Charles Lazarus hired a man named Sy Ziv. The business was growing larger everyday. Lazarus knew that if he wanted to expand his chain of toy stores, he would need sharp, reliable employees to help him manage the operation.

Ziv worked out of Philadelphia as a factory representative for several toy manufacturers. Working together to figure out orders, he and Lazarus became very well acquainted. Lazarus could see that Ziv knew a lot about toys and would fit in well with the Toys "R" Us style of merchandising.

A WIZARD IN TOYLAND

In 1958, Lazarus offered Ziv a job. Ziv soon became one of the most important people at Toys "R" Us and one of the most powerful executives in the entire toy industry.

In those early days, Ziv reportedly did everything from buying merchandise from factories to sweeping the floors at night. But for most of his twenty-five years with the company, he was in charge of buying store merchandise and supervised a large group of **buyers.** Because Toys "R" Us ordered such large quantities, Ziv's opinion on whether or not a toy would sell was very important to all the manufacturers who sold merchandise to Toys "R" Us.

Ziv was a very colorful personality and quite outspoken at times. Many stories are told about him even to this day. His opinion was well respected, and he was quite generous with advice to new toy manufacturers and designers. However, he was also known for having a violent temper. He would hurl samples of toys he didn't like against the wall or floor of his office. During his years at Toys "R" Us, Ziv probably broke thousands of dollars worth of sample toys.

Ziv Meets Slime

Mattel, one of the largest American toy makers, invited Ziv to their offices to see a new product that would eventually become the popular Slime. (Slime is basically a sticky green substance made out of petroleum jelly.) The Mattel executives told Ziv that parents wouldn't object to buying Slime because it was washable if children made a mess in the house with it.

To test this claim, Ziv promptly tossed the glob on the rug, ground it into the carpet with his shoe, poured coffee on it, and asked, "Are you sure?"

The Mattel people were quite shocked to see Ziv "product test" Slime on their office rug. But they had come to expect such outrageous acts from Sy Ziv.

When Ziv retired from Toys "R" Us in 1984, he was a very

rich man due to the money he had made by investing in the ompany as it grew. Like many Toys "R" Us employees, Ziv was able to reap large profits from the hard work he contributed to the company's success.

THE HIGH COST OF GROWTH

By 1966, Lazarus had four stores that sold about $12 million worth of toys each year. From his original $2,000 investment, his business had grown to be worth many millions of dollars. Such phenomenal success might have satisfied other people, but it only served to inspire Lazarus to greater goals—more stores, higher sales figures, and a larger **market share.**

Lazarus had purposely chosen an area of retailing with huge possibilities for growth. His four-store chain had made him a multi-millionaire. But Lazarus knew that he had not yet tapped even a small portion of the chain's market potential. He was determined to expand as much as the market would allow.

Toys "R" Us Sold

In order to open more stores and carry out his vision, Lazarus needed to raise **capital.** He decided to sell his four stores to a large retail **conglomerate** called Interstate Stores. In 1966, Interstate bought the four Toys "R" Us stores for $7.5 million and gave Lazarus the job of running them.

Following the purchase of Toys "R" Us by Interstate, Lazarus continued with his plans for expanding the chain. But although his stores were a profitable division of Interstate, other parts of the company were losing money due to poor management and trying to grow too fast. In 1974, Interstate Stores declared **bankruptcy.**

TO THE RESCUE

If Interstate went out of business, Lazarus knew that all he had accomplished for over twenty-five years would be lost. To save his chain of Toys "R" Us stores, Lazarus persuaded the court to allow him to run Interstate during this critical period.

If Interstate was to survive in any form, Lazarus knew that he had to completely reorganize and restructure the company. This was a very challenging time for Lazarus because so much was at stake. He had to make the right business decisions in order to save the company. Any mistakes would be disastrous.

One of Lazarus' first acts as the new president of Interstate was to streamline operations by selling most of the company's non-toy divisions. He was also able to persuade toy manufacturers to extend generous **credit** terms to the Toys "R" Us stores. This made it possible for the chain to purchase a large shipment of toys from a factory, but they would not have to pay for the shipment for many months. Usually, a retailer is required to pay for goods within thirty to sixty days after delivery. But because of its credit terms, Toys "R" Us was able to sell products that had not been paid for yet. This improved the chain's **cash flow** so that it eventually had enough money to pay for the toys it had purchased.

Help from a Computer

Lazarus also had another powerful weapon in his battle against bankruptcy. It was a computer system that Toys "R" Us installed in 1974, after the chain had become a division of Interstate Stores.

The computer system was first developed to keep track of orders and inventory. Before the computer was installed, all information about orders and inventory was recorded and tabulated by hand. Such a simple, manual system might work for a small toy shop, but not for a number of stores.

As the Toys "R" Us chain grew, there were hundreds of items constantly moving into and out of the warehouse. All orders, sales, and movement of goods had to be accounted for, and this had to be done as quickly as possible. The process of recording and tabulating information by hand was slow, unwieldy, and bound to produce inaccurate results.

"Back then [before 1974], we did all the work by hand," Lazarus recalls. "We ordered and counted every toy manually. Reports were written with a pencil." He has also said that this tedious, time-consuming process "was like painting the Golden Gate Bridge. As soon as we finished, it was time to start over again."

During the challenging period of Interstate's bankruptcy and reorganization, keeping track of information—sales, orders, and inventory—was critical to the company's survival. Because the Toys "R" Us computer system provided Lazarus and his staff with accurate, up-to-date information, they were able to make important business decisions that would increase profits and reduce losses at a time when every dollar counted.

Chapter 5

Toys and Technology

Since 1974, the Toys "R" Us computer system has been expanded to keep up with the ever-increasing amount of orders, sales, and inventory. The system has also been expanded to perform many other tasks. Lazarus has called the Toys "R" Us computer system "our greatest competitive edge." He has said that without a computer system, expanding the chain beyond four or five stores would have been impossible.

"There's no question; computers built this company. We deal with toys. But we do it with high technology."

HOW THE SYSTEM WORKS

Presently, the company's central computer is based at corporate headquarters in Rochelle Park, New Jersey. What does this large and complex computer do for a chain of more than 400 stores?

Computers

The first computers were built around 1950 and called "electronic brains." Computers do work like the human brain by taking in information such as words and numbers. This information is called data. They also take in instructions, called programs, for processing the information. Data and programs are stored in the computer's memory. Because the computer does not understand human language, all information is broken down into electronic impulses that flow through different circuits.

Upon command, computers process data at incredibly high speeds, much faster and more accurately than people can. Computers then output processed data on a display screen or on paper as a printout.

Early computers were very large and took up a great deal of space, the whole floor of a building for example. They were highly sensitive to heat and dust, and also were extremely expensive.

Modern computers with their tiny microprocessors, called "micro chips," are much smaller than the early models. They are also far less sensitive to heat and dust, perform functions faster, and cost much less. For these reasons, computers are now found almost everywhere—in businesses, schools, and homes.

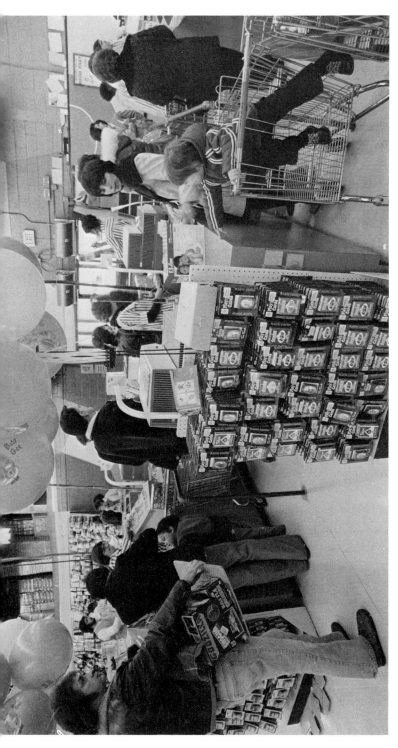

Another important factor in the success of Toys "R" Us is the elaborate computer system that the company uses for recording sales and reordering merchandise. When customers check out, all sales are automatically recorded by an in-store computer, which, at the end of each day, sends the information to the central computer at company headquarters. (NYT Pictures.)

The computerized merchandising system controls the ordering, shipping, and sale of every tricycle, jigsaw puzzle, electric train set, and all other items. Executives at company headquarters can watch the sales and inventory figures for each item and each store with an amazingly high degree of accuracy.

If sales on a new item are slipping, company executives know well in advance when to mark down the price so that they can sell out the stock. All pricing decisions are made at the corporate headquarters and transmitted through the computer system to the individual stores.

Through the computer, all **markdowns** are handled with amazing ease. The price of every item the company sells is in the central computer, which is hooked up to the cash registers at all stores. In the many stores around the country and worldwide, products on the shelves are marked with a universal coding system called a bar code, which is different for every item. When an item is purchased, its bar code imprint is read by the store's computerized cash register, which then asks the main computer for that day's price of the item.

Each transaction is automatically recorded by an in-store computer when an item is sold. At the end of the day, the sales records from each store are transmitted electronically to the central computer at corporate headquarters.

Letting the Computer Decide

The central computer does even more. It practically thinks on its own and makes decisions based on its memory of sales trends and other related information. As Lazarus has pointed out:

Our buyers rely on the computer. If one of them orders 10,000 of a particular toy, the computer might increase that order to 15,000 so that the truck is completely filled to lower unit cost. The computer will then allocate that merchandise to our stores based on past trends and buying patterns. The computer memorized the **marketplace.** It takes into consideration the regional differences and then makes decisions.

Since distribution is closely controlled by the central computer, store managers never have to order merchandise. Lazarus has said that nothing but selling goods is done in the stores. The computer often knows before the store manager does when an individual store in Dallas, Texas, or Seattle, Washington, for example, needs more baseball bats or "Monopoly" games. The information is relayed by the computer to the nearest company warehouse or distribution center, located most often within a day's drive from each store. The toys seem to arrive at a store as if by magic.

The computer keeps track of the number and type of toys shipped to a store and the sales of these toys. For any given toy, the computer system knows how many are in the entire chain and how many are at each store.

Lazarus has said, "I never reach for a pencil. I simply use my terminal, because we have all the information we need in the computer and it's available to anyone who needs it."

Predicting the Toys that Sell

Before the computer age, figuring out which toys would sell better than others was largely a matter of educated guesswork. Product experts, like Sy Ziv, have a knack for seeing the appeal or drawbacks of a new toy. But there is always one unpredictable ingredient in any such guesswork: the consumers' fickle tastes.

"We're very much like the fashion industry," says Lazarus. "Customers tastes are very fickle, and you have to move quickly when they change. Otherwise, you'll be out of business."

Toys "R" Us executives use the central computer's sales information to monitor selling trends. They are then prepared with the right amount of stock when an item seems to take off in the marketplace. For example, when "Trivial Pursuit" suddenly became the hottest game of the season, many toy stores quickly ran out of stock. They couldn't get reorders fast enough to take advantage of the sales demand.

Toys "R" Us, however, had been watching the increased sales activity of "Trivial Pursuit." The chain was one of the few retailers to have ample stock on hand to supply customers, even at the peak of the game's sales. It was also one of the first to see a decline in the game's popularity and reduced its orders before it was stuck with a backlog of stock on a "dead" item.

"You could compare our computer system to a good stock-broker," Lazarus has said. "Any broker can tell you what to buy. But only the best can tell you when to sell."

As Lazarus is quick to point out, it is really the customer's voice that is speaking through the company's sophisticated computer system. "Letting our customers tell us what they want eliminates a lot of guesswork."

Test Marketing to Keep Ahead of Trends

The Toys "R" Us computer can also help company executives plan ahead by keeping track of the **test marketing** of new toys well in advance of the Christmas rush. "We put a toy in our stores at the end of December to test market and take projections on how it will sell the following Christmas," Lazarus explains. "A . . . sampling tells us what is selling, how much it is selling, and where it is selling best. That information is available to us within 12 hours."

Sales figures on the new item are watched the rest of the year for rises and declines. Buyers then know exactly how much to order before the next Christmas season.

WHAT'S NOT ON THE SCREEN

Since 1974, Toys "R" Us has been a leader in applying computer technology to retailing. Lazarus readily admits that his staff is highly skilled in interpreting the central computer's sales reports. "But," he points out, "there's no getting away from the fact that our people are in the stores and watching to see what the customer picks up from the shelf and puts in his basket. They are listening for what we don't have. You won't see that on the screen."

Lazarus is also interested in the "mix" of products in a shopper's basket. "You don't see what the mix is unless you're in the store and you watch the customers check out," Lazarus says. "Then you learn some interesting things about what they like, what they don't like, and what they would have liked, by talking to them."

Chapter 6

The Billion-Dollar Toy Chest

"**I**f you're going to work for yourself," Charles Lazarus once said, "you have to have absolute persistence [continuing to do something despite any problems]. You are not going to do everything correctly the first time you try. You have to learn, and adjust, and try again. . . . And you have to be optimistic [expecting things to turn out well]."

Charles Lazarus' powers of persistence and optimism pulled him through the challenge of reorganizing Interstate Stores and leading the firm out of bankruptcy. Under his direction, the reorganized company recovered from its financial problems in four years. In 1978, Interstate emerged from bankruptcy and was renamed Toys "R" Us.

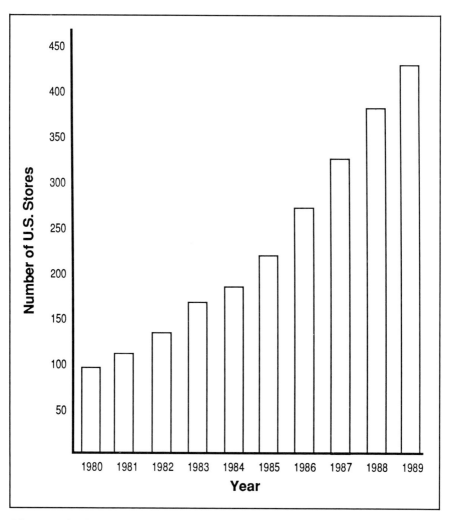

This graph shows the growth in the number of Toys "R" Us stores in the United States from 1980 to 1989.

TOYS "R" US GROWS UP . . . AND UP

Toys "R" Us quickly moved into a period of booming growth that some say is unsurpassed in the history of retailing. In 1980, the chain sold over $600 million of toys, a 24 percent increase over the sales of 1979. In 1975, Interstate **stock** sold for as low as twenty-five cents a share, but by 1981 the new stock had risen to thirty-seven dollars per share.

By 1981 Lazarus had expanded the Toys "R" Us chain to 101 stores, and it was the undisputed leader among toy supermarkets. The closest competitor was Lionel Corporation. Known best for its model trains sets, Lionel sold $207 million in toys in 1980, about one-third the sales of Toys "R" Us.

Toys "R" Us opened about twenty new stores in 1981, bringing the total number of stores to over 120. By 1986, the network of toy supermarkets stretched nationwide, and was ringing up almost $2.5 billion in sales a year. It was clear within the toy industry that competitors like Lionel, Child World, and Kay-Bee Toys had slim hope of ever catching up to Toys "R" Us.

THE INFLUENCE OF A TOY STORE GIANT

Experts on the toy industry have compared Toys "R" Us to a 600-pound gorilla: Where does a 600-pound gorilla sit? Anywhere it wants to.

Having grown into a chain that does billions of dollars in sales each year, Toys "R" Us exerts tremendous influence throughout the entire toy industry. When Toys "R" Us buyers have some comment on a new toy—whether good or bad—toy makers listen.

When a new toy or an entire new line of toys is designed, toy makers invite toy store buyers to see their new products. Sometimes, these new products are previewed and sold at the toy industry's annual trade show, the Toy Fair, which is held every year at the Toy Center in New York City. Other times, representatives of either the manufacturer or Toys "R" Us might visit each other for a special presentation of the new toys. The reactions of buyers to a new toy can determine its success or failure in the marketplace.

Turning Down a New Game

In 1987, one toy company spent $20 million developing a new home video game. The game was designed to compete with the popular "Nintendo" game system, which generally costs about $100. Twenty million dollars may seem like a lot of money to spend in developing a new product, but the toy business is a gambling game with high stakes.

The toy company hoped that its new video game would be the next hot-selling toy at Christmas and easily earn back the $20 million investment. At the peak of their popularity, such toys as Cabbage Patch dolls and Teddy Ruxpin talking bears racked up $300 million to $600 million in sales per year. Nintendo sales, which include the game systems and cartridges, easily approach the one-billion-dollar mark.

But after one look at the new video game, the executives at Toys "R" Us thought it would not sell. Two of their objections were its high price ($200 to $300 for the basic unit) and that the game was not nearly as exciting as Nintendo.

Designing and Developing New Toys

Toys go through a long process of development from the time they are just ideas until they reach the children who unwrap them on Christmas morning. New ideas are created by toy designers, who may be employed by large toy companies or who may work independently and then sell their ideas to manufacturers.

After a manufacturer accepts an idea, a model, or prototype, of the new toy is then constructed. A model can cost several thousands of dollars to build and may be revised after materials, packaging, and other factors are considered. But will children like it? That's the final and most important question.

One way that toy makers determine if children will like a new toy, or if it needs changes to make it more fun, is simply by getting a group of children together and watching them play. One large toy manufacturer has a toy testing room, called Playlab, at their headquarters. Children are invited to Playlab to play with prototype toys as designers watch through a one-way window.

If a new toy can hold a child's interest for more than ten minutes, product designers think that's a very good sign. Toys are also tested in private homes, but designers can judge best if a toy needs changes by observing children at places like Playlab.

> **If a toy fails to interest children, designers make changes, like adding soap bubbles to a toy lawn mower. Then they try it out again with children—and hope they will like it.**

Eventually, the toy company decided to cancel the entire project. Other factors were involved relating to the game's construction, but the reaction of Toys "R" Us buyers played a major role in the tough decision.

The cancellation of the new video game illustrates the powerful influence Toys "R" Us has on the development of new toys. But the chain's influence also works in the opposite way at times. Toys "R" Us can almost guarantee the success of a new product if its buyers like it.

HELPING OTHERS

Lazarus has observed that some of the best products come from "little guys" who need a start. "We look at it all," he has said time and again. Many other retailers, however, will not look at such products and will deal only with big manufacturers. But Toys "R" Us buyers will meet with practically any toy maker—big or small—at any time to see what they have to offer.

Toys "R" Us has also helped to give a new toy idea a chance it may not have had otherwise. When Lewis Galoob Toys showed retailers a new product called "Army Gear," many didn't like it. The line of toys could be changed into different weapons, and the package looked like a wooden crate.

But Toys "R" Us buyers thought the crate-like package was different and would appeal to shoppers. They encouraged Galoob not to change the packaging and ordered the line for their stores. The Army Gear toy line turned out to be one of the twenty top-selling toys that Christmas.

Lazarus has said he likes to think of his relationship with toy makers as a partnership, not as a struggle for the upper hand. Another way he tries to be a partner with toy makers is by sharing sales information from the chain's extensive computer system.

Lazarus has also never forgotten how the generous credit terms of certain toy makers helped his company survive in difficult times. He has been known to help more than one supplier out of debt by prepaying bills to those manufacturers who face financial difficulties.

Chapter 7

Branching Out

Even as Charles Lazarus was planning for more toy supermarkets to be built throughout the United States and abroad, his vision was extending in new directions. Just as he had anticipated the tremendous expansion of the toy market, Lazarus spotted a new area of retailing he thought was about to blossom: children's fashion.

Until recently, children's clothing had been staid and traditional. The emphasis was more on durability than high style. Designs of children's dresses or overalls didn't vary much from year to year, and there was only a handful of manufacturers who made children's clothing.

But little by little, clothes for children became increasingly more exciting. Many big-name designers—such as Ralph Lauren and Laura Ashley—started lines of colorful, high-fashion children's clothes, made with expensive materials and designer details.

The current generation of parents seemed eager to buy the more expensive, fashionable items for their children. It was largely department stores that were reaping the benefit of this new market. No price tag seemed too high for a child's garment with a designer label.

A NEW VENTURE

At the same time, customers in the Toys "R" Us stores saw the few clothing items offered by the chain. These were mostly low-priced items, such as underwear, pajamas, T-shirts, and sweat suits. The customers asked, "Do you have any nicer clothes for children?"

Always eager to serve customer needs, Charles Lazarus had a predictable reaction to that question. He investigated the competition and decided that he could do for children's clothes what he had done for toys: bring the consumer a low price and a big selection. With his methods of low overhead and buying in volume, he believed he could attract a large share of those who were shopping in department stores for children's clothes.

Lazarus' first idea was to sell the children's clothing in the Toys "R" Us stores. However, many of the manufacturers of children's clothes did not want their products sold in the same location with toys.

To overcome this objection, Lazarus used the same successful principles that he had used to create Toys "R" Us. He ventured into a new frontier of retailing: a supermarket for children's clothes. In 1983, he opened the first two Kids "R" Us stores.

KIDS "R" US: THE SAME, BUT DIFFERENT

The first Kids "R" Us stores were experiments in applying the Toys "R" Us sales principles to a new product. Lazarus soon realized, however, that the first two Kids "R" Us stores were too small, so the next stores were bigger, and bigger still after that. He stocked the stores with a wide selection of discount-priced children's clothes and supermarket carts. By 1987 there were 74 Kids "R" Us stores, 137 by 1989, and about 150 by the end of 1990.

Lazarus quickly discovered that there are many differences between selling toys and selling clothes. Selling clothes requires more salespeople to help customers. Clothing also has a much shorter season, or *shelf life,* than toys, and stock needs to be changed in a clothing store every eight to ten weeks. Toys, on the other hand, are not subject to such seasonal turnover.

There is also much more competition selling clothing than selling toys. Customers have many more places in which to shop.

Facing Tough Competition

The competition—mainly department stores—knew how Toys "R" Us had grown to dominate the toy retailing business. They now feared that the same would happen with children's clothes. They responded by cutting prices in their stores on designer or brand-name labels.

According to Kids "R" Us, the competition tried to undermine the new chain in more ways than just by marking down the prices of merchandise. Kids "R" Us claims that several large depart-

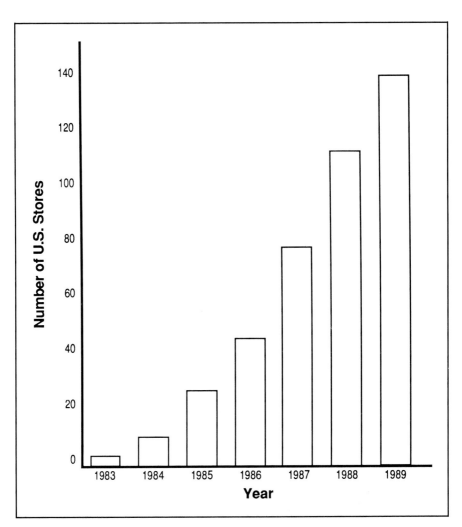

Illustrated here is the growth in the number of Kids "R" Us stores in the United States from 1983 to 1989.

ment store chains tried to pressure a number of manufacturers of children's clothes to stop supplying them to Kids "R" Us.

One way the department stores might have done this was to tell a manufacturer that they would not order his products unless he dropped Kids "R" Us as a client. It is against the law, however, to interfere with a business in this way, which is called *restraint of trade.* But in 1988, Kids "R" Us had to sue one department store chain for restraint of trade, claiming that the department store had persuaded a children's swim suit manufacturer not to sell to Kids "R" Us.

With its large number of stores, there is now no doubt that Kids "R" Us dominates the children's clothing business as much as Toys "R" Us dominates the toy business.

Chapter 8

A Global Strategy

Throughout Charles Lazarus' career, he has always managed to position himself on the forefront of untapped and growing markets in retail sales. He once said that he did not go into business with a specific goal in mind, only great ambition and energy. By 1982, there were almost 150 Toys "R" Us stores and Lazarus was about to open the first Kids "R" Us stores. To most observers, there didn't appear to be any new worlds left for Charles Lazarus to conquer.

Where could Lazarus lead his company next? His standard question had always been, "What does the customer want?" But now he asked himself, "Where are there more customers who want the same kind of stores as my toy and children's clothing stores?"

The answer was simple. It was time for Lazarus to mark out a global strategy.

FOREIGN EXPANSION

The first move for Toys "R" Us beyond the borders of the United States was into Canada. The first Canadian stores were opened in 1984, gradually increasing to 27 by 1990. Singapore was chosen as another international site when Jopie Ong, the director of an investment group in Singapore, persuaded Lazarus to become his partner and open stores in Asia.

At about the same time, Toys "R" Us stores were also opened in England, where many people call them outdoor stores. This is because no retailer had ever sold so many outdoor play items—like sandboxes and swimming pools—in one place before. Other stores soon followed in West Germany, Hong Kong, France, and Malaysia.

In 1984, there were five international Toys "R" Us stores. By 1986 there were twenty-four, fifty-two by 1988, and over seventy by 1989. The expansion of the toy chain overseas reflects the new trend towards world trade and the growth of international corporations.

Toys "R" Us, however, is one of only a few American retailers to move its business overseas in a successful and effective way. Its purchasing of toys from foreign manufacturers had provided the company with the experience it needed to deal with international operations.

Problems in Japan

Like its first association with Jopie Ong in Singapore, Toys "R" Us continues to find partners abroad who also have experience in retail store operations. In Japan, Toys "R" Us signed a joint venture

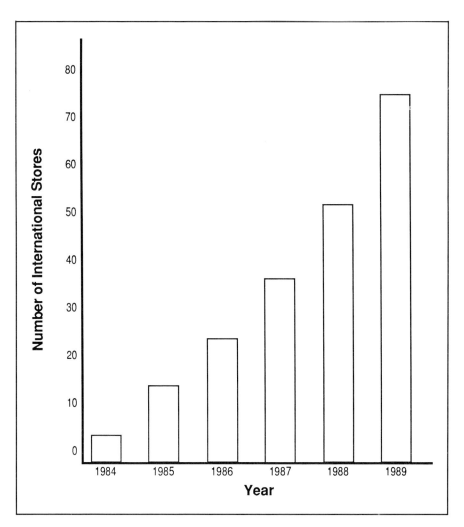

This graph dramatically illustrates the growth in the number of foreign Toys "R" Us stores from 1984 to 1989.

As part of its global strategy, Toys "R" Us has expanded into many foreign countries. The sign over this new store in Koblenz, Germany, says, "Now Open!" (Toys "R" Us.)

agreement with the fast-food empire, McDonald's, to open a combined Toys "R" Us-McDonald's store in 1991.

But because of the many restrictions on foreign companies doing business in Japan, Lazarus foresees some obstacles to opening a number of stores there. Nevertheless, he is optimistic that all problems eventually will be resolved. His firm's success in Japan, Lazarus believes, will pave the way for other American companies to tap the big Japanese consumer market.

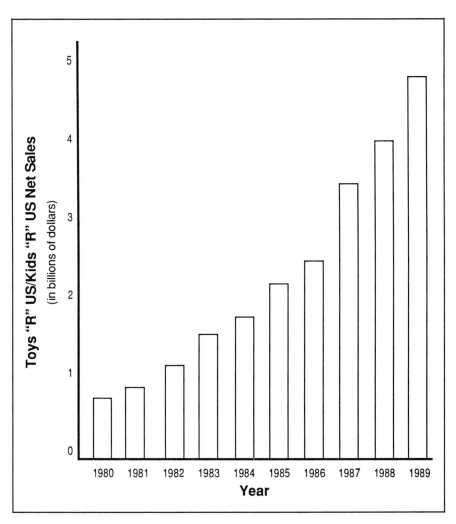

Shown here is the growth in the net sales of all Toys "R" Us and Kids "R" Us stores throughout the world from 1980 to 1989.

Operations Overseas

The overseas stores are set up just like the Toys "R" Us stores in the United States. All stores abroad are hooked up to the central computer at corporate headquarters. And rather than sending in an American manager, the company always hires local country managers and trains them. The country manager then hires his own team of store managers. Local knowledge is considered to be a valuable tool in competing with local businesses.

One major difference between the overseas and American toy markets is television advertising. American children are bombarded with thousands of toy commercials on television. But in other countries, toy makers don't advertise on television as much. Because of television advertising, about 200 major toys must be competitively priced in the United States. But in countries like Taiwan, only about twenty toys are that well known.

Lazarus claims that the firm has emerged as "very interglobal." He cites the cash registers in Hong Kong, which take eight different kinds of currencies, as one example of the firm's international dimension.

LOOKING TO THE FUTURE

As new Toys "R" Us stores open their doors in countries around the globe, the chain also continues to open new stores in the United States at the rate of about thirty per year. The company had once set a goal of 700 stores, but now this figure looks very conservative.

Many business experts believe that the chain will eventually gain between 30 percent to 40 percent of all toy sales in the United States. It is impossible to say how great a share of toy sales world-wide the company can attract. But if Charles Lazarus' track record is any indication, the Toys "R" Us chain will go after the lion's share.

Where will Charles Lazarus lead his firm next? "We can go anywhere there are supermarkets and kids, because we are, after all, a supermarket of toys."

Glossary

bankruptcy The declaration in a court of law of a company's or individual's inability to pay debts.

billing The records that show the amount of money owed to a store, manufacturer, or individual in exchange for the purchase of goods or services.

buyer A person in a retail store or chain of stores who selects and orders merchandise from manufacturers.

capital The money, goods, or property invested in a business to produce an income.

cash flow The movement of money through a business, as when funds received for goods or services are used to pay debts.

credit Time allowed for payment of goods or services purchased by a company or individual.

conglomerate A business corporation made up of many companies that often operate in very different industries.

discount To reduce the price of an item; often used in regard to prices that are lower than the list price (the manufacturer's suggested retail price).

gross revenue The total amount of earnings before overhead costs are subtracted.

inventory The goods or materials on hand in a store, warehouse, or factory; also, the process of compiling a list of such goods (taking inventory).

logo A name, symbol, or other device that distinctly identifies a product or company.

management The people who direct, control, or regulate the various operations of a business.

manufacturer A company that takes raw materials and makes or processes them into a finished product.

markdown The amount by which the original selling price of an item is reduced.

market A specific group of consumers, such as teenagers or women with babies, who will buy certain products or services.

marketplace The world of trade; often refers generally to retail sales, when consumers buy products.

market share The amount of sales an individual company has made of a product in relation to the entire amount of sales by all manufacturers of that product; usually calculated per year and expressed as a percentage. For example, suppose Company X sold five million dollars of "widgets" in 1990 and ten million dollars of widgets were sold nationwide by all widget manufacturers that year. Since Company X sold half of all widgets in 1990, it had a 50 percent share of the widgets market.

merchandise The items that are sold in a store.

merchandising The specific way items are sold in regard to such factors as setting, display, pricing, and service.

net revenue The amount of money remaining after all overhead costs are subtracted from the gross revenue; net revenue is also considered the profit.

obsolescence When an object or service is not used anymore because it is out of date, has lost its usefulness or application, wears out, or breaks.

overhead The operating expenses of a business.

profit The money remaining from selling goods or services after all expenses have been subtracted.

retailing Buying goods in large quantities from a manufacturer or other source, then selling them in small quantities to the consumer at a higher price.

self-service A type of merchandising in which customers select items without the aid of a salesperson and then pay for them at a check-out counter.

stock A certificate of ownership in a company.

system An established procedure or step-by-step method of performing a task, such as the procedure a cashier follows when ringing up a customer's purchase.

test marketing Seeing how well a new product will sell before manufacturing or ordering it in large quantities.

wholesale The sale of goods in large quantities, usually for resale by a retailer.

Index